A CENTURY of
EDINBURGH

To Mabel
all my love
mamie
xx

The Royal Mile threads its way through the heart of the Old Town of Edinburgh from the Castle down to the entrance to the Canongate, 1976. The height of the Old Town tenements, created by building on the slopes from the Lawnmarket and High Street to the old Nor' Loch on the north and the Cowgate on the south have always been a feature of Edinburgh. St Giles' Cathedral sports its distinctive crown spire, restored for the twenty-first century, while the Tron Kirk is enclosed in scaffolding. There have been many changes in the street since 1976, including the construction of the Crown Plaza Hotel, known for many years as the Scandic, and the restoration or reconstruction of many buildings on the south side of the street below the church. (*The Scotsman Publications*)

A CENTURY *of* EDINBURGH

Hamish Coghill

HAMISH COGHILL

SUTTON PUBLISHING

First published in the United Kingdom in 2000 by
Sutton Publishing Limited · Phoenix Mill
Thrupp · Stroud · Gloucestershire · GL5 2BU

British Library Cataloguing in Publication Data
A catalogue record for this book is available from the British Library.

ISBN 0-7509-2627-9

Front endpaper: Colinton Sunday School picnickers pack into two barges at Stoneyport, near Slateford, for their trip on the Union Canal, 1909. The canal is being upgraded as part of a millennium project to reopen the waterway from Edinburgh to Glasgow. (*Currie District Local History Society*)

Back endpaper: The drive to provide housing is exemplified in Oxgangs as multi-storey blocks soar above the 'temporary' prefabs which filled a gap immediately after the Second World War, 1961. There are still some occupied prefabs in the city.

Half title page: A three-year-old Leith girl is dressed as a Newhaven fisherwife for a local gala.

Title page: 'They came as a boon . . .': one of the great advertising slogans of all time for the Waverley Pen. The signs have now gone from the Blair Street premises they adorned for much of the century.

 Published in association with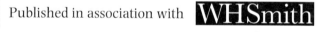

Typeset in 11/14pt Photina.
Typesetting and origination by
Sutton Publishing Limited.
Printed in Great Britain by
The Bath Press, Bath.

Out on a limb, 1997. Tree lopping in a city garden means strict safety measures for the man with the saw.

Contents

Foreword

BY THE RT HON. ERIC MILLIGAN, LORD PROVOST OF THE CITY OF EDINBURGH

Lord Provost Eric Milligan

Edinburgh's golden age is generally held to have been in the eighteenth and early nineteenth centuries at the time of the Scottish Enlightenment when a unique group of individuals such as David Hume, Adam Smith, Allan Ramsay and Sir Henry Raeburn brought recognition to the city with their creative achievements. However, in the course of the twentieth century, particularly the last fifty years or so, Edinburgh was transformed from being a douce, conservative and complacent city into a thriving, dynamic, cosmopolitan capital city, with the promise of a new golden age on the horizon.

The great catalyst for this transformation was the establishment of the Edinburgh International Festival after the Second World War, bringing the city alive every August and providing the impetus for a burgeoning cultural scene. The Fringe, the Tattoo and the other festivals we are now so familiar with, followed on after that making Edinburgh a great festival city.

Wherever you look in Edinburgh, you cannot fail to notice the spread of new developments with a new conference centre, business premises, government buildings, hospitals, museums, art galleries, theatres and tourist attractions already having been built or well on the way to completion. There are plans to regenerate whole areas of the city such as the waterfront and the south-east wedge of the city, and generally speaking Edinburgh people are enjoying a higher quality of life than ever before.

In the final year of the century, Scotland's first democratically elected Parliament was established in the city making Edinburgh a more complete capital city than ever before.

Edinburgh ended the twentieth century as a city on a roll. The momentum of the last few years will take the city forward for a number of years yet. As we stand at the dawn of this new millennium, I feel a great optimism for Edinburgh where the city can look forward to a new golden age, an age that promises so much and an age where I feel that Edinburgh will at last be able to reach its full potential.

Britain: A Century of Change

Two women encumbered with gas masks go about their daily tasks during the early days of the war. (*Hulton Getty Picture Collection*)

The sixty years ending in 1900 were a period of huge transformation for Britain. Railway stations, post-and-telegraph offices,
police and fire stations, gasworks and gasometers, new livestock
markets and covered markets, schools, churches, football grounds,
hospitals and asylums, water pumping stations and sewerage plants
totally altered the urban scene, and the country's population tripled with
more than seven out of ten people being born in or moving to the
towns. The century that followed, leading up to the Millennium's end in
2000, was to be a period of even greater change.

When Queen Victoria died in 1901, she was measured for her coffin
by her grandson Kaiser Wilhelm, the London prostitutes put on black
mourning and the blinds came down in the villas and terraces spreading
out from the old town centres. These centres were reachable by train
and tram, by the new bicycles and still newer motor cars, were con-
nected by the new telephone, and lit by gas or even electricity. The shops
may have been full of British-made cotton and woollen clothing but the
grocers and butchers were selling cheap Danish bacon, Argentinian
beef, Australasian mutton and tinned or dried fish and fruit from
Canada, California and South Africa. Most of these goods were carried
in British-built-and-crewed ships burning Welsh steam coal.

As the first decade moved on, the Open Spaces Act meant more parks,
bowling greens and cricket pitches. The First World War transformed
the place of women, as they took over many men's jobs. Its other
legacies were the war memorials which joined the statues of Victorian
worthies in main squares round the land. After 1918 death duties and
higher taxation bit hard, and a quarter of England changed hands in
the space of only a few years.

The multiple shop – the chain store – appeared in the high street:
Sainsburys, Maypole, Lipton's, Home & Colonial, the Fifty Shilling Tailor,
Burton, Boots, W.H. Smith. The shopper was spoilt for choice, attracted
by the brash fascias and advertising hoardings for national brands like
Bovril, Pears Soap, and Ovaltine. Many new buildings began to be seen,
such as garages, motor showrooms, picture palaces (cinemas), 'palais de
dance', and ribbons of 'semis' stretched along the roads and new
bypasses and onto the new estates nudging the green belts.

During the 1920s cars became more reliable and sophisticated as well
as commonplace, with developments like the electric self-starter making
them easier for women to drive. Who wanted to turn a crank handle in
the new short skirt? This was, indeed, the electric age as much as the
motor era. Trolley buses, electric trams and trains extended mass
transport and electric light replaced gas in the street and the home,
which itself was groomed by the vacuum cleaner.

A major jolt to the march onward and upward was administered by
the Great Depression of the early 1930s. The older British industries –

textiles, shipbuilding, iron, steel, coal – were already under pressure from foreign competition when this worldwide slump arrived. Luckily there were new diversions to alleviate the misery. The 'talkies' arrived in the cinemas; more and more radios and gramophones were to be found in people's homes; there were new women's magazines, with fashion, cookery tips and problem pages; football pools; the flying feats of women pilots like Amy Johnson; the Loch Ness Monster; cheap chocolate and the drama of Edward VIII's abdication.

Things were looking up again by 1936 and new light industry was booming in the Home Counties as factories struggled to keep up with the demand for radios, radiograms, cars and electronic goods, including the first television sets. The threat from Hitler's Germany meant rearmament, particularly of the airforce, which stimulated aircraft and aero engine firms. If you were lucky and lived in the south, there was good money to be earned. A semi-detached house cost £450, a Morris Cowley £150. People may have smoked like chimneys but life expectancy, since 1918, was up by 15 years while the birth rate had almost halved.

In some ways it is the little memories that seem to linger longest from the Second World War: the kerbs painted white to show up in the

A W.H.Smith shop front in Beaconsfield, 1922.

blackout, the rattle of ack-ack shrapnel on roof tiles, sparrows killed by bomb blast. The biggest damage, apart from London, was in the south-west (Plymouth, Bristol) and the Midlands (Coventry, Birmingham). Postwar reconstruction was rooted in the Beveridge Report which set out the expectations for the Welfare State. This, together with the nationalisation of the Bank of England, coal, gas, electricity and the railways, formed the programme of the Labour government in 1945.

Times were hard in the late 1940s, with rationing even more stringent

than during the war. Yet this was, as has been said, 'an innocent and well-behaved era'. The first let-up came in 1951 with the Festival of Britain and there was another fillip in 1953 from the Coronation, which incidentally gave a huge boost to the spread of TV. By 1954 leisure motoring had been resumed but the Comet – Britain's best hope for taking on the American aviation industry – suffered a series of mysterious crashes. The Suez debacle of 1956 was followed by an acceleration in the withdrawal from Empire, which had begun in 1947 with the Independence of India. Consumerism was truly born with the advent of commercial TV and most homes soon boasted washing machines, fridges, electric irons and fires.

The *Lady Chatterley* obscenity trial in 1960 was something of a straw in the wind for what was to follow in that decade. A collective loss of inhibition seemed to sweep the land, as the Beatles and the Rolling Stones transformed popular music, and retailing, cinema and the theatre were revolutionised. Designers, hair-dressers, photographers and models moved into places vacated by an Establishment put to flight by the new breed of satirists spawned by *Beyond the Fringe* and *Private Eye*.

In the 1970s Britain seems to have suffered a prolonged hangover after the excesses of the previous decade. Ulster, inflation and union troubles were not made up for by entry into the EEC, North Sea Oil, Women's Lib or, indeed, Punk Rock. Mrs Thatcher applied the corrective in the 1980s,

Children collecting aluminium to help the war effort, London, 1940s. (*IWM*)

A street party to celebrate the Queen's Coronation, June 1953. (*Hulton Getty Picture Collection*)

as the country moved more and more from its old manufacturing base over to providing services, consulting, advertising, and expertise in the 'invisible' market of high finance or in IT.

The post-1945 townscape has seen changes to match those in the worlds of work, entertainment and politics. In 1952 the Clean Air Act served notice on smogs and pea-souper fogs, smuts and blackened buildings, forcing people to stop burning coal and go over to smokeless sources of heat and energy. In the same decade some of the best urban building took place in the 'new towns' like Basildon, Crawley, Stevenage and Harlow. Elsewhere open warfare was declared on slums and what was labelled inadequate, cramped, back-to-back, two-up, two-down, housing. The new 'machine for living in' was a flat in a high-rise block. The architects and planners who promoted these were in league with the traffic engineers, determined to keep the motor car moving whatever the price in multi-storey car parks, meters, traffic wardens and ring roads. The old pollutant, coal smoke, was replaced by petrol and diesel exhaust, and traffic noise.

Fast food was no longer only a pork pie in a pub or fish-and-chips. There were Indian curry houses, Chinese take-aways and American-style hamburgers, while the drinker could get away from beer in a wine bar. Under the impact of television

Punk rockers demonstrate their anarchic style during the 1970s. (*Barnaby's Picture Library*)

the big Gaumonts and Odeons closed or were rebuilt as multi-screen cinemas, while the palais de dance gave way to discos and clubs.

From the late 1960s the introduction of listed buildings and conservation areas, together with the growth of preservation societies, put a brake on 'comprehensive redevelopment'. The end of the century and the start of the Third Millennium see new challenges to the health of towns and the wellbeing of the nine out of ten people who now live urban lives. The fight is on to prevent town centres from dying, as patterns of housing and shopping change, and edge-of-town supermarkets exercise the attractions of one-stop shopping. But as banks and department stores close, following the haberdashers, greengrocers, butchers and ironmongers, there are signs of new growth such as farmers' markets, and corner stores acting as pick-up points where customers collect shopping ordered on-line from web sites.

Futurologists tell us that we are in stage two of the consumer revolution: a shift from mass consumption to mass customisation driven by a

Millennium celebrations over the Thames at Westminster, New Year's Eve, 1999. (*Barnaby's Picture Library*)

desire to have things that fit us and our particular lifestyle exactly, and for better service. This must offer hope for small city-centre shop premises, as must the continued attraction of physical shopping, browsing and being part of a crowd: in a word, 'shoppertainment'. Another hopeful trend for towns is the growth in the number of young people postponing marriage and looking to live independently, alone, where there is a buzz, in 'swinging single cities'. Their's is a 'flats-and-cafés' lifestyle, in contrast to the 'family suburbs', and certainly fits in with government's aim of building 60 per cent of the huge amount of new housing needed on 'brown' sites, recycled urban land. There looks to be plenty of life in the British town yet.

Edinburgh: An Introduction

Edinburgh entered the twentieth century as a fairly small, conservative city, proud of its position as Scotland's capital, prosperous in business, and hiding many of its sins in the deepest parts of the Old Town. Edinburgh is a city of two parts, even today – the historic Old Town, the heart of the medieval town which spread from the Castle Rock down to the Palace of Holyroodhouse, and the Georgian splendour of the New Town with its broad boulevards, sweeping crescents and fine town houses.

Anyone returning to Edinburgh after 100 years would recognise part of the place at least. The Royal Mile is still the heart of the town, and those who proclaim Princes Street as the principal thoroughfare are, to my mind, backing a Johnny-come-lately – it is a mere stripling of slightly more than 200 years. Castlehill, Lawnmarket, High Street and the Canongate (together with Abbey Strand they make up the Mile) have seen the history of the ancient town unfold, and through its narrow closes and wynds a bustling life still whisks, taking the resident and visitor back through time.

The century was a time of struggle for Edinburgh, a time when some problems like housing and social exclusion were tackled only half-heartedly at one stage. As recently as the forties and fifties families were still struggling in the slums to clothe the youngsters properly, and many a laddie in the Pleasance could not go to a Scout meeting or another function because it was not his turn to wear the shoes he shared with his brother.

It is easy in the prosperity of 2000 to forget that half a century or less ago there were still shared toilets on the landings of dark, sunless tenements. Hot water was a luxury not enjoyed by many, and weekly visits to the public baths were not for swimming, but for a hot bath.

The century opened quietly enough with Queen Victoria still on her throne, and her death in 1901 brought a feeling of great grief. People went about their business in the genteel prosperity of the New Town and some of the plusher areas of suburbia like Morningside or Colinton, still surrounded by countryside before the post-First World War housing boom sprawled across green fields and cherry orchards. The little villages, once

holiday retreats like Juniper Green or Davidson's Mains, were set to be swallowed up into the city proper as the boundaries expanded.

The First World War brought a fervour of excitement as men queued to join up. The Heart of Midlothian football club's first team enlisted to a man, and recruiting offices did a brisk trade.

The heart was wrenched from the city, however, by one fateful event more than any other. In the early hours of May 1915 the train carrying men from the 7th Leith Battalion The Royal Scots was in a head-on collision with a local train at Gretna Junction. The death toll was 214 officers and men and 13 civilians. Edinburgh in general and Leith in particular were shaken to the core. Hardly a family in Leith, then still a separate burgh, did not lose a son or relative in that disaster. There was excitement, too, the night in 1916 that a German Zeppelin swooped across the city indiscriminately dropping high explosives and incendiaries and leaving a trail of destruction and several deaths. Civilian casualties in the city may have been light, but like many other Scottish towns and villages the war memorials tell their own poignant story.

Ready for a make-over, 1992. The old Empire Theatre in Nicolson Street awaits a multi-million pound transformation into the Edinburgh Festival Theatre, a venue capable of housing opera and ballet for the International Festival.

The inter-war years were times of social unrest as well as change. The port of Leith lost its independence and was swallowed up by its neighbour in 1920, despite a huge majority in a plebiscite against the merger with Edinburgh. The last cable cars were replaced by electric tram cars in 1923 and during the General Strike of 1926 students volunteered to drive the trams in days which brought violence to the streets. Some years later, in 1933, thousands of hunger marchers swept into the city to highlight the problems of the unemployed and the poor housing in which many were forced to live.

Although the Forth Estuary was the target for one of the first German air attacks of the Second World War in 1939, Edinburgh again escaped comparatively lightly, with only one major raid in 1941 which destroyed Leith Town Hall and other property.

In Edinburgh slum clearance saw new 'schemes' built at Craigmillar and Niddrie, and the spread of private bungalow land as the city expanded rapidly. The traditional industries like brewing and printing were big employers; shops like Darling's and Binns and Patrick Thomson

Princes Street, 1920s. A tram car heads along its rails down the famous thoroughfare. Cars were allowed to park on the roadway then, and the open charabanc is maybe a forerunner of the tourist buses which throng the city today. The much-loved trams were finally withdrawn from the increasingly congested streets in November 1956.

flourished. St Cuthbert's Co-operative Society seemed to have shops on every corner, and paid a handsome dividend to their customers. The 'store', as St Cuthbert's was known, and the Leith Provident Co-operative Society were to lose their separate identities later in the century as the co-operative movement stumbled, and a giant ScotMid was formed by a series of amalgamations. But the 'divvy' days are fondly remembered by Edinburgh folk who can still rattle off their store or provy number.

A shaft of inspirational light came with the launch of the Edinburgh International Festival in the gloom after the Second World War. The 1947 event was in many ways an act of faith and its impact took many by surprise. But inevitably the Festival has always had critics, despite its outstanding success in projecting the city. Only in the 1990s was the old Empire Theatre transformed into an opera house after years of wrangling and a series of debacles which left Edinburgh for many years with a notorious 'hole in the ground' in Castle Terrace.

Parliament's base, 1999. The site in Holyrood for the new Scottish Parliament building. Controversy rages over the design and costs of the project. The site between the Canongate and Holyrood Road was formerly the headquarters of Scottish and Newcastle Brewers. The Parliament currently meet in the Church of Scotland Assembly Hall at the top of the Mound.

If the F word was for festival, then the D word was for demolition. By the 1950s slum housing was a major problem, and when a tenement in the Pleasance collapsed – the Penny Tenement which the owner had offered to the Town Council for one penny to take it off his hands – the council were galvanised into action and the new housing programme, already in place after the Second World War, was stepped up. Huge areas of the Pleasance, Dumbiedykes, Greenside, parts of Stockbridge, the Kirkgate and the Citadel in Leith and many other areas were demolished – and many claim Leith in particular and the wee fishing village of Newhaven have never been the same, with the heart ripped out of the areas and families dispersed from their familiar surroundings to far-flung estates on the city's outskirts.

St James' Centre in the city centre was also swept away, and in the place of Georgian tenements, designed by James Craig, the planner of the majestic first New Town, rose the concrete monstrosities of a New St Andrew's House and a shopping centre. The good news for 2001 is that plans are in place to demolish New St Andrew's House, which at one time housed the Scottish Office, and build a new headquarters for the Royal Bank of Scotland on its site.

The 1960s architecture sticks out like a sore thumb and some of it has been 'softened' or even, in the housing estates, cleared away.

Walking down a childhood street, however, a person would miss many of the corner shops, the once-familiar cinemas replaced in the main by multiplexes, and family businesses ousted by chain stores, although the queen of Princes Street – Jenners – still stands firm. Only two breweries are left, but there is an abundance of bars, restaurants and hotels. Dance halls like the Palais at Fountainbridge, frequented by the young Sean Connery, and the Plaza are no more.

On the sporting front the city hosted two Commonwealth Games – in 1970 and in 1986. The premier football clubs Heart of Midlothian and Hibernian survived proposals for their amalgamation and are still at their respective grounds of Tynecastle and Easter Road. At the magnificently transformed Murrayfield Scotland's rugby team still manage to beat England in the only game that really matters!

No visitor to Edinburgh today can fail to note its busyness. As a major tourist centre, boosted by a host of festivals spread over the year, a Hogmanay celebration unequalled anywhere, attractions like the former Royal Yacht *Britannia* and Our Dynamic Earth bring in the crowds. The industries may have changed, many of the names of the great printing houses, for instance, are but memories – but there is new wealth. New buildings for the burgeoning financial sector abound, and there is a booming housing market.

For a while the city endured the notoriety of being known as the Aids capital of Europe, and it still suffers, like any other city, from a

Edinburgh in the 1990s, and eating out is the big thing. Restaurants and bars, like these in the High Street, found customers enjoyed eating and drinking al fresco.

drugs problem. There are beggars on the streets, and waifs and strays gather in the city's graveyards for shelter and solace from a bottle.

But what other city in Britain has an old volcano in its midst and a castle on a rock which gives it such an unforgettable skyline? The good folk of Edinburgh maybe take their city too much for granted, but don't talk to them about traffic, parking or the 'blue meanies' who book erring motorists.

No one knows what changes the twenty-first century will bring, but I hope this book captures some of the past 100 years.

A Leisurely Start

Family home, *c.* 1900. A woman and child outside their home in Horse Wynd in the Canongate. The girl is well turned out and is wearing boots, unlike many of her poorer contemporaries in the area who would run bare-footed round the streets. The houses in Horse Wynd were eventually replaced by brewery offices. (*Old Town Oral History Project*)

Changing times, 1904. Mr King, the coachman at Curriehill House on the outskirts of Edinburgh, makes a splendid figure with his horse and carriage. But he is in for a big change with the arrival of the automobile. He was sent for training on his new charge and had to change his top hat and riding jacket for a new cap and uniform befitting the well-trained chauffeur. (*Currie District Local History Society*)

In service, *c.* 1900. Many Edinburgh men and women found employment working in domestic service in the town houses and mansions on the city outskirts. The staff at Malleny House, at Balerno, now part of the city, would have worked long hours for their low wages and keep. (*Currie District Local History Society*)

The hard way, *c.* 1900. No washing machine in every house in those days! These women had to boil the water and then pour it into a wooden tub where the clothes were scrubbed and rinsed and wrung out by hand, before being hung on the drying line. (*Currie District Local History Society*)

A day at the seaside and a youngster enjoys a pony ride on Portobello beach, *c.* 1900. The sands were a great attraction for the folk of Edinburgh who flocked there to enjoy the summer attractions, including a pier which was taken down during the First World War. There is a fun fair on the beach, and whatever happened to the pony on the sand – is it just having a wee lie-down after a hard day carrying boys and girls? (*CSV Scotland Local History Project – Mrs A. Stephen*)

Places to relax. As a great brewing centre, it seemed likely that Edinburgh would have many public houses, and these are two typical turn-of-the-century establishements. The Miller family ran the pub above at the corner of York Place. The staff make an impressive sight behind the highly polished bar top, with a glistening and well-stocked gantry behind them. Not quite so salubrious is Inglis' bar at the top of Cockburn Street, but again the staff are well turned out. Both pictures show the pump handles for serving the beer. (*Above: CSV Scotland Local History Project – Nettie McKay; below: Old Town Oral History Project*)

Working men, *c.* 1900. Beards are the order of the day for four out of five workmen on a site in the Old Town. Every man is also wearing a cap and waistcoats are *de rigueur*. The mason holds his mallet while the plasterer also carries the tools of his trade. The unidentified building they are working on is probably still standing today. (*Old Town Oral History Project*)

Not a car trip, *c.* 1905. It was the fashion to have a formal family photograph taken in one of the many studios in the city. You could choose various scenes – an Edinburgh background, a sandy beach or like this a new-fangled motor car. This family group looks somewhat apprehensive, but there is little chance of this horseless carriage roaring off at 4 miles an hour! (*CSV Scotland Local History Project – Neil Scott*)

Village blacksmiths, 1901. These sturdy blacksmiths at Corstorphine smiddy were still very busy men, serving a mainly agricultural area before the open countryside was swallowed up by an advancing city. The notice nailed to the door is for a forthcoming local election in the parish of Corstorphine. Note, too, the advertising bills – suits for 21 shillings and trousers for half that price. (*Currie District Local History Society*)

Cup winners, 1906. Members of Leith Athletic Football Club pose proudly with their trophies after winning the Scottish Qualifying Challenge Cup in the season 1905/6. The officials almost outnumber the players, while the trainer J. Duckworth is ready to rush on to the field and revive injured players with his flapping towel. Leith Athletic were formed in 1887 and finally wound up in 1957. (*CSV Scotland Local History Project*)

Quarrymen, 1900s. The need for stone for building an expanding town and for road bottoming and other purposes meant that the quarries round Edinburgh were busy places employing many men. Here the workers at Ravelrig Quarry pose for the photographer, all with the exception of the blacksmith Jimmy Finlay wearing the distinctive flat caps of the period. One of

the men in the middle row sports a splendid white moustache which must have needed brushing out daily to rid it of the quarry dust. At one time quarryworkers in Edinburgh were encouraged to grow beards and moustaches to help filter out the grime and prevent it from getting into their lungs. (*Currie District Local History Society*)

Off to the church outing, 1908. It's Sunday School picnic time, and these youngsters at Juniper Green are all set. The horse's harness is burnished, and the girls wearing their best clothes and fine bonnets are already on board the cart. The laddies with their little caps look very serious, and while some sport brightly polished boots others come from poorer families and are going to run around in their bare feet. (*Currie District Local History Society*)

Country station, *c.* 1908. The way to travel into the outlying areas was by train, quietly chugging from the Caledonian railway station at the end of Princes Street out through Slateford and Colinton Dell towards Colinton station and the villages of Juniper Green and Balerno beyond. Porters were on hand to look after the luggage, and at this time many families took a house in Colinton for the summer months. The line was finally closed in the 1960s, although passenger traffic ceased in the 1940s. (*Currie District Local History Society*)

Market man, *c.* 1910. The local shops played an important part in community life in Edinburgh. James Christy stands outside his 'famous Southside Market' in East Crosscauseway where he sold the finest quality hams, eggs, butter and cheese at lowest prices. His well-stocked vegetable stall was another attraction for customers, and apples would be stored in the wooden barrels. (*Old Town Oral History Project*)

Flower girls, *c.* 1910. A blooming good show! The florist's shop run by K. and J. Low in the Canongate brought a dash of colour to the drab surroundings of many slum properties in the area. Sprays, bouquets and cut flowers were offered as 'cheapest in town' and the assistants in their blouses and long dresses are a far cry from modern florists. The children seem to be dressed in their best for the photograph. (*Old Town Oral History Project*)

Early Boy Scouts, 1910. The recently formed 29th East Edinburgh Scout Troop are on parade under Mr Fulton, their Scoutmaster. The Scout movement was founded by Robert Baden-Powell in 1908 and quickly attracted many young lads in Edinburgh. Their distinctive broad-brimmed hats were a feature of early uniforms, and these boys are also carrying their staffs. Many of the youngsters in the photograph would certainly answer their country's call when the First World War broke out, when their early Scout training would have been invaluable. (*Edinburgh Scout Museum*)

31

Praise the Lord!, *c.* 1910. The Moody and Sankey hymns ring round the old buildings and people passing in the Canongate would know that the Edinburgh City Mission were holding an open-air meeting in Whitehorse Close. The wooden staircases are a thing of the past as the Close went through a modernisation later in the century and the houses, once verging on slums, became among the most sought-after houses in the Royal Mile. (*Old Town Oral History Project*)

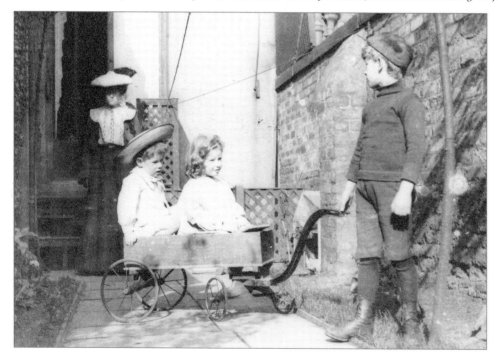

Garden scene, *c.* 1908. The children play in safety in their walled garden in Edinburgh under the watchful eye of an Edwardian lady – their mother? The boy sports long shorts over his stockings while giving the other children a hurl in the guider. (*CSV Scotland Local History Project – Joan Dougan*)

Paying the Price

Back from the trenches, 1917. Too familiar a sight on the streets of Edinburgh and towns and villages throughout Scotland during the First World War – the wounded soldier in his distinctive blue overalls as he fights his way back to health. David Scott poses for a formal picture on a break from his convalescent stay in Flora Stevenson's School at Comely Bank. Like many other premises it was pressed into service to receive the hundreds of wounded sent home to recuperate. (*CSV Scotland Local History Project – Neil Scott*)

Edinburgh's Princes Street is dressed to mark the Coronation visit of King George V and Queen Mary to their Scottish capital, 1911. A 'Loyal and Happy Welcome' says the hoarding alongside the special stand erected outside St John's Church at the West End. Open-topped cable cars are running along the street, and the centre line between the rails shows how they were propelled by powerful mechanisms housed in the tramway depots. The visit was a very happy event for the city, when most people did not imagine the horrors of war which were shortly to erupt. (*Currie District Local History Society*)

A hero's return, 1914. King's Prize rifleman Sergeant James Dewar of the 4/5th Battalion, The Royal Scots returns home in triumph after his markmanship success at Bisley. He and members of his family toured round the village of Juniper Green in their open car, which bears its registration number above the engine. His success would undoubtedly encourage many local men when recruiting started. Certainly there was no shortage of volunteers to make use of the Malleny ranges (below) on the slopes of the Pentland Hills. While the markers stand behind the riflemen, onlookers are kept well back behind a rope. (*Currie District Local History Society*)

Remount depot, 1914. Boy Scouts were among those who rushed to assist in the First World War. Here they are helping out at a remount depot in the city, helping grooms to take water and feed to the military horses which were ridden by officers and by cavalrymen. The Scouts were also used to groom the horses and muck out the stalls, and their work became increasingly valuable as their elders went off to war. (*Edinburgh Scout Museum*)

Village baker, 1914. The horse and van were still very much part of the way of life, and John Graham stands by his vehicle outside his Juniper Green shop. He would deliver over a wide area on the west of Edinburgh, while his shop was a focus in the village itself, which was a popular spot for holidays or a day out for people living in the city centre. (*Currie District Local History Society*)

Marching off to war, 1914. Young recruits, flanked by regular soldiers, watched by anxious families and excited children, march off behind the local band and the recruiting sergeant. There was no shortage of volunteers when war was declared and the recruiting offices in Edinburgh were flooded with young men wanting to do their bit. Older men watch with a sense of foreboding as the cream of the country head off, while the small boy in the foreground shows a fine line in fur-collared coats. (*Currie District Local History Society*)

Military duty, 1914–18. Many of the Edinburgh and Leith men joined up with The Royal Scots (The Royal Regiment). Known as Pontius Pilate's Bodyguard because the regiment are the First of Foot in the British Army, The Royal Scots raised many battalions during the war, and above are officers and men of the kilted 9th Battalion – The Dandy Ninth. With thousands of troops mustering and being trained in the city, and others passing through, the Military Police were kept busy. Below are a group of the police soldiers based at Redford Barracks. (*Currie District Local History Society*)

Life goes on, 1916. Three assistants at the Macvitties, Guest baker's shop in Comiston Road, Morningside, look happy enough, but many young women in Edinburgh lost their sweethearts in the war. With so many men away, the womenfolk had to shoulder the domestic responsibilities and many had to find work to keep the family home going. Macvitties had several shops throughout the city, and there's little doubt that customers and staff would swop the latest news from the front as bread and cakes were sold. (*CSV Scotland Local History Project – Nettie McKay*)

A needed break, 1914–18. Soldiers longed for a spot of leave and a chance to relax away from the noise and squalor of the trenches. And there was nothing better than the welcoming kiss and smile of a sweetheart and the comfort of some home life for a few precious days. This group was photographed on a day out at Roslin on the outskirts of the city where even in the quiet countryside you could not escape entirely the clutches of war. For at Roslin was a gunpowder factory where the workers (below) made materials which found their way into the explosives which were hurled at the enemy on the European killing fields. (*CSV Scotland Local History Project – Neil Scott*)

Three little maids, 1913. There are loaves aplenty stacked in the shelves of this baker's shop in Leith and the girls wear their overalls to protect their dresses from the flour. Leith was then a separate burgh, not being swallowed up by Edinburgh till 1920, much to the disgust of most Leithers who voted strongly against the merger – or takeover as they saw it. (*CSV Scotland Local History Project*)

Cub excursion, *c.* 1916. These members of the 54th Edinburgh Cub pack had an expedition to Blackford Hill with their Akela and her assistant. The Cubs are still the younger members of the Scout movement, and these lads would have been versed in the stories of Mowgli and the lore of the jungle. The little green caps lasted a long time as part of the uniform. (*Edinburgh Scout Museum*)

Counting the cost, 1919. Scenes like this were typical as the frightful cost of the First World War was realised. War memorials throughout the city were unveiled, listing the names of local men who did not come home from the action. Many women also died on active service, serving as nurses and in other capacities. The crowd who gathered at Currie to pay their

respects when the war memorial was dedicated would have had bitter memories when the heroic days of marching off to war were remembered. Those who served and returned joined the service, grateful that they had survived. (*Currie District Local History Society*)

Height of fashion, *c.* 1920. These two men sported thistles in their buttonholes when they posed in an Edinburgh photographic studio on 'Scotch and Irish Day'. The boots are lace-up, the best suits are spick and span, but there are no collars and ties. And beneath the very floppy caps, there's no question about being politically correct and dumping the fags for the picture! (*Old Town Oral History Project*)

Drawing Breath

By the fireside, *c.* 1920. Granny Law sits scanning her paper. The old lady, probably in her eighties, does not need spectacles to read the close print by the light streaming through the window of her cottage. She is comfortable in her wicker basket chair and the pot is warming by the side of the coal fire in her range. The kettle is ready to be put on the swee and swung on to the flames. (*Currie District Local History Society*)

Drouthy characters, *c.* 1920. They stand outside an Old Town pub which does not look too salubrious. Edinburgh's old streets were always cobbled, making a rough ride for early cyclists, and causing a lot of horses to slip and skid. Modern motorists have no great love for the old granite causies these days either when they become slippery in the rain. (*Old Town Oral History Project*)

Taking a breather, 1920. Women staff from McLagan and Cumming, the Warriston Road printing firm, leave their desks for a while to pose in the garden. Many women got their jobs during the First World War and were accepted in the printing trade when the men they replaced returned. Edinburgh was a major printing centre but a once great industry has shrivelled in the city. (*CSV Scotland Local History Project – Neil Scott*)

Pony parade, *c.* 1920. Mr Wyllie's ponies were much in demand for gala and Infirmary pageant days in various parts of Edinburgh. Based at Currie, the animals earned their keep by appearing in the pantomime *Cinderella* in the city and in Glasgow in alternate years. On this occasion they are pulling the pageant queen's coach at Juniper Green. (*Currie District Local History Society*)

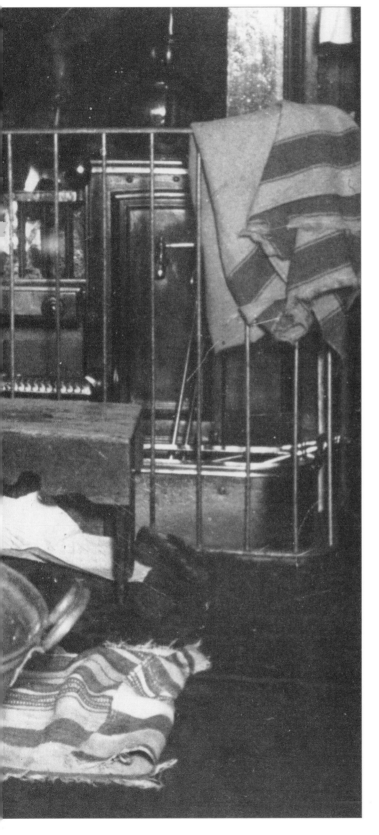

Bath night, 1920s. A scene which might have been captured in many a house in Edinburgh. With no running hot water, the kettles and pots would be boiled over the coal fire, the tin tub brought down from the peg on the kitchen door, and the children given a good scrub, probably once a week, in front of the hearth. Mothers saved water by washing the children two at a time, and the towel over the fireguard will be cosy for the youngsters when they are thoroughly clean and ready for drying. Many housewives took great pride in the appearance of their grates which provided warmth and a welcoming focus of the living room, and they were blackleaded regularly and carefully polished. (*Currie District Local History Society*)

All the latest, *c.* 1920. Mr Macpherson stands in the doorway of his shop in Shandon with the newspaper boards proclaiming the latest news in the respective journals. Women 'won' the right to vote after the First World War, although it was restricted to those over thirty years of age. In 1928 the ballot was extended to all women at the age of twenty-one. (*Currie District Local History Society*)

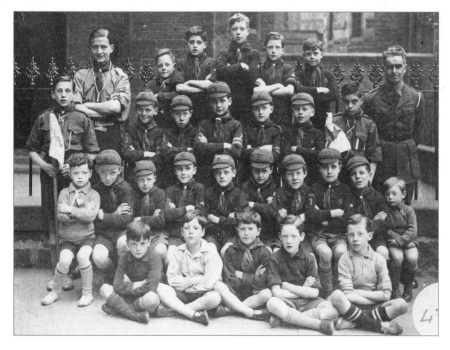

School's out, 1931. And for their leisure activities these boys joined the 158th Craiglockhart Wolf Cub pack based in St Ignatius School in Glen Street, Tollcross. The new recruits don't have their uniforms yet, or were they just passing and decided to join their pals for the picture? (*Edinburgh Scout Museum*)

Local shopping, 1920s style. The Miller family ran the Kingsknowe Dairy in McNeill Street, Viewforth, from 1915 until 1965. It was a genuine corner shop and operated as a grocery as well as providing fresh milk for its customers. Many little shops went out of business when the owners retired or competition became too fierce, but there has been a recent boom in Edinburgh in shops open till late at night to serve their neighbourhood. (*CSV Scotland Local History Project*)

Graduation day, 1923. These students at Edinburgh University graduated Master of Arts and the women wear their mortar boards with pride. With three universities and a university college in the city thousands of students now graduate every year, and graduation day sees a flood of proud graduates walking the streets in gown and degree hood.

Brush and shine, *c.* 1920. Well-brushed shoes maketh the man, and the shoeshine man in Princes Street probably did good business. Like many returning from war he may have found a job difficult to get, and turned to shoe polishing to make a few pennies.

A garden outing, 1929. This group travelled to Inverleith to visit the Botanic Garden and sample one of Edinburgh's great attractions. The car hood is down so it must have been a fine day, although the ladies seem to be taking no chances with their long coats – and the men are wearing sweaters. (*CSV Scotland Local History Project – Barbara Jeffrey*)

A young man's joy, 1931–2. Alexander Kendall proudly shows off his Royal Enfield motorbike beside Bull's Close in the Canongate. No question of helmets or leathers in those days of uncrowded streets and light traffic. (*CSV Scotland Local History Project – Peggy Kendall*)

Fund raising, *c.* 1920. The annual Royal Infirmary pageant to raise cash for Edinburgh's great hospital attracted many floats for the procession. They came from a' the airts and this Currie float was pictured in the Old Town on its way to Holyrood Park to join in the fun. Thousands of pounds were raised in the event which drew huge crowds of onlookers for the dressed lorries and vans. (*Currie District Local History Society*)

Time for a swim, *c.* 1933. Swimming styles have certainly changed since this group met at Portobello Baths on the Promenade, and the off-the-shoulder style of costume prevailed. The baths were a very popular venue for local men who would find coaching in their club as well as recreational swimming. (*Maureen Runciman*)

Class of 1929. These youngsters lived in the tenements of the Lawnmarket at the top of the Royal Mile and round about, and went to Castlehill School for their three Rs – reading, 'riting and 'rithmetic. The wee lad with the dummy looks as if he joined his brother or sister for the day. (*CSV Scotland Local History Project*)

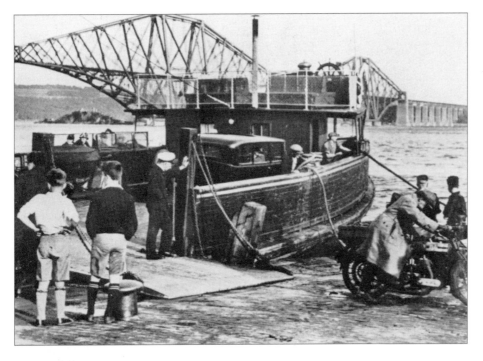

Over the sea, 1933. A trip to Fife and back made a day out for Edinburgh folk, and the ferry boats carried cars, motorbikes, cyclists and pedestrians across the Forth from Queensferry to North Queensferry. The ferries were discontinued with the opening of the Forth Road Bridge in 1964. (*Old Town Oral History Group*)

A royal occasion, 1935. King George and Queen Mary are on hand during their jubilee visit to Edinburgh for the hand-over of a new horse ambulance to the Scottish Society for Prevention of Cruelty to Animals. The presentation took place in the grounds of Holyrood Palace where the King and Queen were staying. (*Currie District Local History Society*)

Family group, 1936. A mother and her children pose on the outside stairs of their home in Baberton Avenue. It is summer, the children are sockless and from the flag the wee lad's carrying it looks as if they could be on the way to the local gala day parade and celebrations. (*Currie District Local History Society*)

Welcome to the world, 1938. The cots are ready in the sunshine on the ward balcony at the Elsie Inglis Hospital, waiting for mothers to bring their newly born babies out for a bit of fresh air. One mother is nursing her child in the chair and the nurses are ready to lay the other children in the cots. Elsie Inglis was a great medical pioneer in Edinburgh, fighting for the rights of women to practise medicine. She died during the First World War when she ran field hospitals. (*CSV Scotland Local History Project – Estelle MacLeod*)

Newsman, 1939. James Seager, who became Editor of the *Edinburgh Evening News*, seated at his desk in the Market Street office, and aware that the storm clouds were looming over Europe.

Home builders, 1934. These plasterers and labourers worked for James Miller, one of Edinburgh's best-known building firms, and were in McDonald Road, off Leith Walk, when the photographer called. During the inter-war years there was a big growth in bungalow building, which spread across once rural parts of the city. Developers advertised (below) the type of house you could get – for a mere £650 – and listed four areas in which the style was being built – Kingsknowe, Greenbank, Corstorphine and Craigentinny. Note the weekly mortgage repayment. (*Right: CSV Scotland Local History Project – Mrs E. Cravan; below: Currie District Local History Society*)

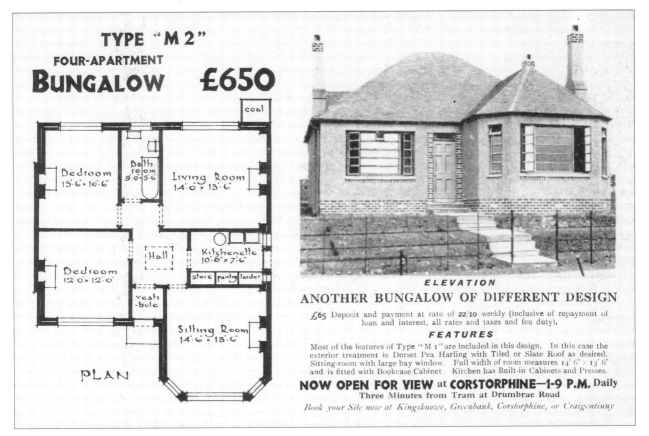

TYPE "M 2"
FOUR-APARTMENT
BUNGALOW £650

coal

Bedroom 13'6" × 10'6"

Bath room 9'0" × 5'6"

Living Room 14'0" × 13'6"

Hall

Kitchenette 10'6" × 7'6"

store | pantry | larder

Bedroom 12'0" × 12'0"

Vesti-bule

Sitting Room 14'6" × 13'6"

PLAN

ELEVATION

ANOTHER BUNGALOW OF DIFFERENT DESIGN

£65 Deposit and payment at rate of 22/10 weekly (inclusive of repayment of loan and interest, all rates and taxes and feu duty).

FEATURES

Most of the features of Type "M 1" are included in this design. In this case the exterior treatment is Dorset Pea Harling with Tiled or Slate Roof as desired. Sitting-room with large bay window. Full width of room measures 14' 6" × 13' 6" and is fitted with Bookcase Cabinet. Kitchen has Built-in Cabinets and Presses.

NOW OPEN FOR VIEW at CORSTORPHINE—1-9 P.M. Daily
Three Minutes from Tram at Drumbrae Road

Book your Site now at Kingsknowe, Greenbank, Corstorphine, or Craigentinny

Ready and willing, 1939. Auxiliary fireman John Tweedie, stationed at Angle Park, was one of the men who volunteered once the call went out for recruits to the Fire Service as war approached. Others joined ARP or the LDV, later the Home Guard. (*Currie District Local History Society*)

Pulling Their Weight

Carefree for some, *c.* 1940. The sirens may have sounded, and the first bombs fallen on Edinburgh and Leith, but young Peter Bottomley can still find some fun. He is hanging from the lamppost of one of the gaslights in the Dumbiedykes. War time meant that windows had to be blacked out to prevent any light showing at night, Anderson shelters were built in many gardens, and often basements were bricked up to make bomb-proof shelters. (*Old Town Oral History Group*)

Dad's Army, 1940. Officers of the Home Guard based at Holyrood pictured in front of the Royal Family's Scottish home, the Palace of Holyroodhouse. The Home Guard used the adjoining park for training with rifle range firing, map reading and other exercises designed to provide an effective fighting force if the enemy ever invaded Scotland.

The real thing, 1940. Enough to make a Scotsman cry as one million gallons of whisky go up in flames after a German bomb was dropped on the Caledonian Distillery at Dalry. Hundreds had to leave their homes as the fire spread to tenements in Duff Street, Springwell Place and Downfield Place. (*Currie District Local History Society*)

Supplying the goods, *c.* 1940. These carters and their horses are gathered at the LMS rail company depot in Lothian Road, beside the Caledonian station. The Clydesdale horses proved a boon when rationing affected vehicle petrol supplies, and they certainly pulled their weight in the war effort. (*Old Town Oral History Group*)

On the farm, 1943. The men went off to far-flung lands to wage war, and many of the young women joined the Land Army. Edinburgh woman Maisie Brand shows her tractor-driving skills on a farm at Hawick. The Land Army proved an invaluable force in helping out on farms with staff shortages. (*CSV Scotland Local History Project*)

Every little helps in wartime. These Girl Guides got hold of a pony and plenty of sacks and went off to pick sphagnum moss on the slopes of the Pentland Hills for the war effort. The moss was very effective for dressing wounds, being both antiseptic and highly absorbent. (*Currie District Local History Society*)

Roll out the barrel, *c.* 1940. The breweries managed to keep going and beer continued to be produced in places like Campbell Hope and King's Brewery, where George Fleming and his workmates are steaming the casks ready for filling. (*Old Town Oral History Group*)

A Granton grocer, 1946. The war may be over, the bonfires burned in the street and the victory parades held, but there is still rationing in the shops. Food is tight, and sweeties for the bairns still need precious coupons. But the town struggled on, and folk looked to the future. (*CSV Scotland Local History Project*)

Time to start enjoying things again, 1946. Workers from Parsons Peebles (above) take time off for a picnic at Gullane sands, and make it a family affair by bringing along the children. Special efforts were also made in many homes to make sure a child's birthday did not go unnoticed. The party (below) was held in a Granton house where despite shortages you can be sure there was enough food for everyone, and probably a wee sweetie treat as well. (*CSV Scotland Local History Project – Barbara Guthrie and Ella Rattray*)

A sweet foursome, 1948. These girls from Duncan's chocolate factory at Powderhall were very popular. Jean Riley and her pals could always rustle up the odd chocolate sweetie or so. The Beaverhall Road factory used to send out lovely smells of hot chocolate across the area, but, alas, it no longer exists. (*CSV Scotland Local History Project – Jean Riley*)

A gala celebration, 1949. The queen and her court look resplendent at the Davidson's Mains and Cramond Gala in Davidson's Mains Park. The children are from the local schools and a lot of work has gone into making the girls' dresses and the boys' costumes. Throughout Edinburgh events like this were given fresh impetus after the war as people wanted to lift themselves from the gloom.

They had bottle in 1947. This cheery bunch are the bottling squad at Lorimer and Clark's Caledonian Brewery in Slateford Road. The brewing industry has been one of the hardest hit in the city, with only two major breweries still existing, along with some pub breweries and microbreweries. (*Caledonian Breweries*)

On parade, 1949. The Edinburgh Battalion of the Boys' Brigade hold their annual Founder's Day parade along Princes Street. Taking the salute is the Brigade Secretary Stanley Smith, son of the Boy's Brigade founder, Sir William Smith. The granite setts have long since gone from Princes Street, along with the Commercial Bank and many other shops. (*Edinburgh, Leith and District Battalion, Boys' Brigade*)

Boy Scout gathering, 1950. The Inch estate was the site for a huge Corroboree of Edinburgh Scouts where they welcomed Lord Rowallan, the Chief Scout. The Scout leaders in the front row with the Chief are Jack Cuthill, Betha Younger, Sir Hugh Rose, John Crawford and Norrie Lind Weir. The camp was the last event staged on the estate which was turned over to housing, although Inch House and park are still a community asset. (*Edinburgh Scout Museum*)

Entertaining in the late 1940s. And they continued to do so for many years after that, the Edinburgh Harmonica Band under their leader Gordon McFeeters. The band played at charity and community events throughout the city and brought a lot of enjoyment. (*CSV Scotland Local History Project – Eric Grainger*)

Staff party, *c.* 1949. Staff of the New Picture House in Princes Street have a night out with their partners in Stewart's Ballroom at Abbeymount. The New was in Princes Street from 1913 until May 1951 when it closed, and the site is now occupied by Marks & Spencer. (*CSV Scotland Local History Project – Peggy Kendall*)

Hauling Down . . .

The face of Edinburgh's housing in the fifties. Councillor Frank Stewart surveys rundown and condemned housing in St Patrick Square on the Southside. People were living in houses which in some cases were little more than hovels and the Town Council, urged on by many concerned people, started to tackle the massive postwar housing problems.

It's fun time in 1951. Fancy dress is the order of the day for the contestants at Portobello Gala. One little girl is in her rose costume, another is a soap packet, while the wee boy is dressed as a once-familiar character on the Edinburgh streets – an onion, or ingin', Johnny. The name was given to the Frenchmen who came from Brittany with their strings of onions and pedalled their way round town on big black bikes selling their vegetables round the doors. They were generally based in a warehouse in Leith during their stay. Below is the view the Gala court got of the audience as they made up the platform party. Such events generally attracted a good turnout, although sadly some of them have withered because of lack of support. (*Maureen Runciman*)

Coronation Day, 1953. These worthy ladies of the Canongate – Cannygoshuns – gathered for a celebration in Chessel's Court. There were many parties in or around June, and streets were decorated and tables brought out into the roadway for the occasion. The young Queen and the Duke of Edinburgh visited Edinburgh shortly after the Coronation and received a rapturous welcome. (*Old Town Oral History Group*)

Queen for a day, 1953. Rosalind Rattray knew what is was like to be a monarch, if only for an afternoon at her gala day in Crewe Crescent. She was crowned and with sceptre and orb presided over her court on an occasion she will never forget. (*CSV Scotland Local History Project*)

Making whoopee, early 1950s. After helping to organise the gala for the kids, what better way to round off the celebrations than with a gala dance and the chance to unwind and meet friends? Many of this happy Portobello group made it a formal occasion with black tie and even some in tails, while the ladies have on their best dresses. (*Maureen Runciman*)

Sunday night is music night, 1950. The venue is the Capitol cinema in Manderston Street, Leith, with Freddy Riley in full voice. Concerts were a feature of some Edinburgh picture houses, and this one seems to be held in one of the small rooms, not in the cinema itself. The Capitol was one of the victims of the TV age and became a bingo hall in 1961. (*CSV Scotland Local History Project – Freddy Riley*)

Party time, 1958. These young lassies proudly did their turn at a backgreen concert party in Bingham Road. Children always used to like putting on concerts, sometimes to raise money for charity, sometimes just for a bit of fun for the people living round about. And it was always a good way for newcomers to meet new friends when they moved in. (*CSV Scotland Local History Project*)

Sporting '50s, and there's a touch of glamour at Portobello Pool from the ladies on the diving boards who appear to be modelling swimming costumes through the ages. In front is Mrs C. Sutherland showing off her newly gained life-saving badge, at that time one of only three people in the United Kingdom with such an award. Skating was another popular pastime, and Rosalind Rattray is displaying her skills on the ice some years later in 1956. The Haymarket Ice Rink is now closed, although the rink at Murrayfield still caters for skating enthusiasts. (*CSV Scotland Local History Project – Mrs C. Dickie and Ella Rattray*)

Town Council, 1953. The berobed councillors and bailies of the City of Edinburgh pose for an official picture in the City Chambers. In the centre of the front row is Lord Provost James Miller, who was later knighted, and went on to carve a place in municipal history. He is the first, and so far only, man to be Lord Provost of Edinburgh and Lord Mayor of London. The

Lord Provost and councillors no longer wear their red robes, and the Lord Provost's ermine-trimmed outfit is in the city's Huntly House Museum. The last man to wear the robe was Lord Provost Norman Irons, between 1992 and 1996.

Military entertainment on a lavish scale. The Edinburgh Military Tattoo, which celebrated its golden jubilee in 2000, has been an outstanding success in its annual performances on the Castle Esplanade. The massed pipes and drums never fail to thrill Scot and visitor alike, and the show is now watched by countless millions on TV throughout the world. (*Edinburgh Military Tattoo*)

On church parade, late 1950s. The 1st Battalion, Argyll and Sutherland Highlanders, march back to barracks from Colinton Church, led by their Shetland pony mascot Cruachan. Edinburgh was a garrison town throughout the twentieth century, with soldiers stationed either in the Castle, or at Redford or Dreghorn Barracks. From the length of the coat the boy on the corner is wearing, it was a hand-me-down from his big brother!

Housing desolation, 1955. People were so desperate for accommodation that they moved into former service huts at Lochinvar (above) and Duddingston Camps, living in near squalor. But at least they had a roof over their heads. The bulldozers moved in to clear away the buildings, and many of the residents were rehoused by the Town Council which was starting to embark on a major house-building programme.

Ready for the bulldozer, 1956. The bleak streets off the Pleasance where housing conditions were miserable and many families lived in damp and dark housing. There were shared toilets on the landings, roofs had missing tiles and windows were broken, but the landlords would not pay for repairs. Carnegie Street (left) and Dalrymple Place (below) were typical of many areas of old tenement property in the city which had to come down. Many of those moved out regretted the loss of the familiar community spirit, but most were glad to shake off the last of their slum times.

A vision of the 1950s. Edinburgh University came up with a master plan (right) to create a whole new campus round the lovely George Square, then almost 200 years old. They wanted modern buildings round the Old College (foreground) in South Bridge and the McEwan Hall, and the plan envisaged the campus stretching across Nicolson Street and into the Pleasance. The sketch (below) shows the detail of what might happen if a pedestrian square was formed outside the McEwan Hall, and that has been achieved, but after demolishing many of the lovely townhouses in George Square and building a new library and two tower blocks the scheme ran out of steam – much to the relief of many Edinburgh citizens.

Sweet charity, 1957. These 'girls from St Trinian's' are students Mary Allan and Dorothy Watt on Edinburgh University Students Charities Week when hundreds of them dressed in fancy costumes and asked the citizens to open their wallets and purses and give for charity. At one time many ridiculous stunts were conceived like pushing a penny along Princes Street by noses and go-cart races down Middle Meadow Walk. It was all good fun. The students also organised a procession of floats along Princes Street and 'Border Raids' to Peebles and other Border towns.

. . . And Putting Up

May Day, 1960. For many years before and since people have climbed Arthur's Seat, the old volcano in Holyrood Park, to greet the dawn on May Day. The minister of the Canongate Kirk takes a service on the summit to mark the occasion, and tradition says that if you wash your face in the dew that morning you will be beautiful for the next year.

The city from above, 1960. The shape of the west end of Edinburgh has altered dramatically and the old Caledonian railway station and yards have long since been swept away. Financial buildings on the Exchange Square, the International Conference Centre and the Sheraton Hotel, together with the Western Approach Road, cover the site now. Gone too from the mid-foreground is the former Rutland (later Gaumont) cinema, while the Usher Hall, the domed building below the castle, has undergone a multi-million pound renovation. (*The Scotsman Publications*)

The battle goes on, 1960. Arthur Street, which became known as one of Edinburgh's bleakest slums, was renowned for its steep cobbled roadway leading to the boundary of Holyrood Park. For the residents the impending demolition was a merciful release. And in Greenside, off the foot of Leith Street, in 1961 a similar fate awaits these houses. The site is now occupied by a multi-storey car park and is awaiting development above ground level.

Still waiting, 1962. Virtually the whole Dumbiedykes area was zoned for slum clearance, and this woman in Heriot Mount is showing neighbours the bit of stonework that has just fallen off. It's not a bonfire piled up in the street but wood to erect barriers (below) round the property before demolition. The corner shop struggles on and at night the gas lamp still shines out amidst the gloom. Major rebuilding took place in Dumbiedykes and it is still mainly a residential area.

Going up, 1963. A tower block in Couper Street, Leith, rises above its neighbours as the old port gets a new look. Many tenements were ripped down in Leith and families who had centuries-long roots in the area were dispersed to new council housing estates on the periphery of the city. A community was again destroyed, many felt, as they remembered the slogan 'Aince a Leither, aye a Leither'.

Time for a news break, 1962. Members of the editorial staff of the *Edinburgh Evening News* gather round Chief Reporter Lewis Simpson's desk for a presentation to a departing colleague. A *News* photographer, needless to say, is on hand to take a picture, and in those days he had to screw a large bulb into his flash gun. The paper's Editor Bob Cairns is on the left.

Poor oot, 1962. The young girl on the right dashes forward as the bride and groom follow an old Scottish tradition of hurling coins from the window of their wedding car. Small silver and copper were the norm and there was often a scramble among youngsters waiting for the chance to grab a share of the money.

Farewell to steam, 1962. The branch line from the Caledonian station to Balerno was closed to passenger traffic in 1944, but commercial trains, serving the mills on the Water of Leith, continued until it was finally decreed that the line must shut under Dr Beeching's surgery. So one last passenger excursion train made a sentimental trip along the line which saw the 'Balerno Express' puff happily for many years.

Conservationists' disgust, 1962. George Square, started before the New Town, was irreparably damaged under Edinburgh University's development plans. The David Hume building is already soaring over the eighteenth-century townhouses which are themselves to vanish from the south side of the square as the new university library is built. Conservationists lost a long and bitter battle to keep the square intact.

Coal delivery, 1964. India Place in Stockbridge with the adjoining Mackenzie Place was another self-contained community living in sub-standard housing, and while there is still life in the street it is not going to last much longer in these particular houses. They are for sweeping away, to be replaced by blocks of flats.

Good for a blaw, 1965. Edinburgh Scout pipers have a practice skirl before Beating the Retreat at the Ross Bandstand in Princes Street Gardens. Such occasions always attract big crowds, and the bandstand has now been renamed the Ross Theatre where top bands play at the city's Hogmanay celebrations.

Gamesmanship, 1962. The future Lord Provost Herbert Brechin (centre) along with Councillor Magnus Williamson (right) present Edinburgh's case for hosting the 1970 Commonwealth Games at a Games Federation meeting in Kingston, Jamaica. Mrs Brechin accompanied her husband. In due course the Games came to the city and proved successful beyond anyone's wildest dreams: they were the 'Friendly Games'.

Demolition corner, 1967. The buses and other traffic had a tight squeeze getting in and out of Inglis Green Road from the main Slateford Road, so a road widening scheme was brought in to clear away buildings in both streets, to put in a large roundabout, and open up the junction. And so another old part of Edinburgh disappeared. (*Currie District Local History Society*)

Can I do you now, sir? – seventies style. The Cub and Scout Bob-a-Job Week caught the public imagination and the lads got up to all sorts of pranks to raise publicity for the Scout movement's big fund-raising effort. These Cubs decided they could earn some cash at the Zoo at Corstorphine by offering to take the animals for some exercise. (*Edinburgh Scout Museum*)

Communion, 1978. The Right Rev. Dr Peter Brodie, the Moderator, officiates at communion at a session of the General Assembly in the Assembly Hall. The annual gathering in May of ministers and elders of the Kirk continues in the hall, which is also the temporary home of the Scottish Parliament.

On parade, 1978. William Ross, former Secretary of State for Scotland, served as Lord High Commissioner – the Queen's representative – at the General Assembly. And traditionally he inspected the Boys' Brigade Guard of Honour in Parliament Square before the Assembly service in St Giles' Cathedral. (*Church of Scotland*)

Completed in 1970 and reviled ever since, the St James Centre continues to dominate the east end of town. But while the shopping centre will continue, the hideous New St Andrew's House is coming down, and a new headquarters building for the Royal Bank of Scotland will rise in its place.

Playtime, 1970s. A concrete boat with a gangplank and funnels is provided for the children living in new flats at Muirhouse to enjoy. Not the same as swings and roundabouts, but a youngster's imagination will soon have him or her making wonderful voyages of discovery across the seas.

A Nation Again

City life, 1962. This familiar figure tramped the city streets for many a year with his distinctive helmet covered by a balaclava, his welly boots and carrying his bags. Always clean and tidy, rumour had it he was a man of learning and means. He often left piles of pennies for children to pick up. In his later days he moved into a hostel; he is now dead.

Papal visit, 1982. Thousands thronged the streets for a glimpse of Pope John Paul II when he visited Scotland and held mass for the faithful at Murrayfield Stadium. His Popemobile made a triumphal trip along Princes Street.

New Year, 1982 – Vietnamese style. The Vietnamese community in the city celebrated their New Year with a display at the Mound. Swirling banners and dragons made a complete contrast to the traditional Scottish event with its pipes and whisky drinking.

Miners' Gala Day, 1980. The Gala, heading to Holyrood Park, was one of the great trade union events in Scotland, but is now no more. Up to 100,000 miners and their families rallied for a day of speeches and entertainment in the Park, and latterly in the Meadows.

Horse power, 1982. And time is running out for the milk horses which carried out deliveries for St Cuthbert's Co-operative Association. The 'store' horses were much loved, and were fed carrots and other tit-bits as they pulled the milk carts round town. They were replaced by a mechanised fleet of trucks, and now Scotmid (St Cuthbert's successor) have no horses. But there are still horses in Edinburgh and those below kick up their heels in a field near Liberton Tower.

Empty canal, 1984. A lengthy stretch of the Union Canal at Fountainbridge was drained to trace a leak. The canal was formed to link Edinburgh to Glasgow, via Falkirk, and now a millennium scheme is under way to make the canal navigable again so that boats will be able to travel to Glasgow once more.

Gone to the dogs, 1989. Powderhall Stadium is another of the sporting venues which has gone. It closed in 1995 after 120 years of use for various activities – greyhound racing, athletics, football and speedway racing among them. Now it is a building site.

Vanished scenes, 1980s and 1990s. Fire in 1991 destroyed the Palace Hotel which stood at the corner of Castle Street and Princes Street. The demolition job was a huge task taking many weeks. From the ashes rose the only completely new building in Princes Street in the decade.

The old red stand at Murrayfield rugby ground came down in 1993 as the stadium was redeveloped. This picture shows the new east stand. The stadium has now been completely rebuilt to make one of the best sporting grounds in the country.

A last bargain from the Lyon and Turnbull Lane sale, February 1999. Many a home has been furnished with furniture bought in the sales. The last was actually held in a warehouse in Thistle Street Lane and was an emotional affair for the regulars.

Festival boom time. The Stockbridge Festival is a community event which goes from strength to strength and one of the most popular events is the duck race in the Water of Leith. You pay for a little plastic toy duck which is numbered, and the one that goes furthest wins the prize. Did the wee girl win in 1993?

The Festival Cavalcade, organised by the *Edinburgh Evening News,* has become the popular start of the Edinburgh Festival. Now headed by Tattoo performers, it attracts more than 100,000 spectators to Princes Street; and in 1983 one of the attractions was these saloon girls from an American fringe company.

Dancing in the streets, 1998. The Festival brings plenty of fun to the streets as well as great music and drama in the concert halls and theatres, and the Fringe performers have the use of a traffic-free High Street for three weeks to give open-air performances. These young dancers step lively in the hope of attracting audiences to their evening show.

Games saviour, 1986. So the late Robert Maxwell boasted as the Commonwealth Games organisation got into a muddle and Edinburgh looked like facing major embarrassment as the city hosted the great sporting event for a second time. The now-disgraced newspaper proprietor showed the Queen the Press Centre where Edinburgh Scouts and Guides provided a messenger service. (*Edinburgh Scout Museum*)

Every dog has his day, 1996. Spot, like Greyfriars Bobby, has a place in Edinburgh lore on this manhole cover in the West End. When the original cover for a coal chute into a basement cellar was damaged, Alan and Kathy Jowett had a new one specially made and engraved.

Frogs galore, 1990s. This sign appears in the springtime in Holyrood Park warning motorists to watch out for frogs crossing the road to St Margaret's Loch. No driver has been eaten by a giant frog – yet!

Parking, 1997 style. It's not got so bad yet that you have to park in the Water of Leith. This car was abandoned in the Water of Leith beneath Colinton Bridge and polluted the river for several weeks before it was removed.

Above: Animal warning, 1990s. This sign in rural Edinburgh may not be in the Highway Code but the message is clear. There is still a green belt round the city, although developers clamour to eat into it, and there are still a remarkable number of farms like this one near Balerno.

Right: Dog watch, 1990. Someone's always watching when you stroll the streets of Edinburgh and this dog leaning out of a Canongate window is just keeping an eye out for his pals. A canine version of Neighbourhood Watch.

Ripe for redevelopment,1983. The Universal Household Stores are missing upper storeys in this stretch of the High Street. Now the Museum of Childhood, a fascinating attraction run by the council, has a new home on this site, rebuilt to enhance the Royal Mile.

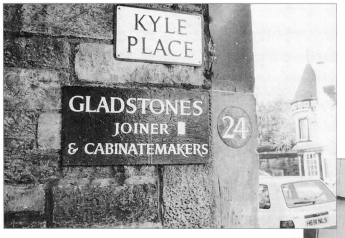

Scottish education, 1998. Well, spelling is not everyone's strength, and the joiner's sign is a talking point in the lane off Montrose Terrace. At least the signwriter did not stick in an apostrophe before the s.

Message for the 1990s. This shop in Cockburn Street reflects the new mood of irreverence of the late twentieth century. Cockburn Street, off the High Street, was revamped in the '90s and is a tourist route between the Old and New Towns.

First lady, 1988. Eleanor McLaughlin made history when she became the first and so far only woman Lord Provost of Edinburgh. She served a four-year term at the same time that Susan Baird was Lord Provost of Glasgow – a unique double.

A hand of freedom, 1997. Nelson Mandela, then President of South Africa, received the Freedom of the City from Lord Provost Eric Milligan at a private ceremony in the Caledonian Hotel. Mr Mandela was in the city for the Commonwealth Heads of Government meeting and declined a public ceremony for the occasion. Lord Provost Milligan has a special place in the city's history too: he is the only person in recent times to be serving a second term as Lord Provost.

Royal tasting, 1999. The Duke of Edinburgh visited the Caledonian Brewery in Slateford Road and sampled their champion beer. The managing director Russell Sharp (right) led a buy-out from Vaux in 1987, and despite a disastrous fire which resulted in the destruction of the maltings in 1994 the brewery continues to win awards for its ales. (*Caledonian Brewery*)

The changing street, 1990s. Gone is Joe Pullar, the news vendor, who had a stance for many years at the corner of George Street and Frederick Street. A great character who had served in The Royal Scots, he knew all his regulars and always had a cheery word even in the vilest of weather.

The best-known street character for the past decade and more. Cosmo, with his Marks & Spencer bags, strolls completely unmoved through the joyous crowds who gathered to cheer the Scottish Cup winning Hearts team in 1998. He is originally from Italy.

Hello, hello, hello. What's happened to our police boxes then? Many of them have been sold off and turned successfully into little coffee stalls. This one at the top of the Middle Meadow Walk has been in business for some years now, and is popular with visitors to the nearby Royal Infirmary.

No 2000 dunce he. David Hume's statue in the Lawnmarket is 'adorned' with a traffic bollard, but the wise man of the Edinburgh eighteenth-century enlightenment was certainly no slouch. His statue was placed outside the new High Court building in 1997.

The Stone's back, 1996. It was St Andrew's Day, 30 November, when the Stone of Destiny returned to the Scottish capital. Escorted by members of the Royal Company of Archers the Stone was welcomed at a service in St Giles' Cathedral before going to Edinburgh Castle where it now lies with the Honours of Scotland. The Stone on which the kings of Scotland were crowned at Scone was removed by Edward I and placed in Westminster Abbey.

Remembering Princess Diana, 1997. Edinburgh held a special service at the Ross Theatre in Princes Street Gardens on the day of Princess Diana's funeral. Like many others throughout the land, Edinburghers felt a great wave of sorrow at the news of Diana's untimely death, and people queued to sign a book of condolence in the City Chambers.

On the ice, 1998. Open-air skating in East Princes Street Gardens was introduced as a Christmas and New Year attraction and was an instant success, although one Edinburgh winter was so mild that the ice started to melt. It is one of the attractions designed to entertain visitors flocking into the city for the Christmas and Hogmanay celebrations.

The big bang. Since the nineteenth century the one o'clock gun has been fired from the ramparts of Edinburgh Castle, causing visitors to jump and citizens to check their watches to see if the gun is on time. Many tourists visiting the Castle clamour to see the daily (except Sunday) ceremony.

Fireworks Edinburgh. Dramatic firework displays have become a feature of Edinburgh in the nineties, with the Festival fireworks concert and Hogmanay. There is no better backdrop for the display than the Castle high on its volcanic rock in the heart of the city.

Down and out, 1996. He sleeps quietly under an archway in the Cowgate. He is one of the men of the streets for whom the council are setting up hostels and drop-in centres to ease the plight of the homeless and those in need of support.

Hogmanay, 1999. And if you have 200,000 people cramming into the city centre for the celebrations, you need extra toilets to meet the demand. Streets off Princes Street are lined with portaloos for the occasion. Edinburgh's Hogmanay has now become one of the biggest events of its kind in the world.

The great day, 1 July 1999. The Scottish Parliament is in being again after almost 300 years. The Queen, the Duke of Edinburgh and Prince Charles travelled in an open coach with mounted escort up the Royal Mile from Holyroodhouse to the Assembly Hall for the historic moment when Her Majesty declared the Parliament

A city of carvings and plaques. This one in the Royal Mile commemorates a tenement collapse in the nineteenth century. Many people were buried in the masonry but one man urged his rescuers to 'heave awa'' and lift the rubble to free him.

Acknowledgements and Picture Credits

Thanks to the following who provided photographs and much assistance in the compilation of this book:

Caledonian Brewery, Ron Davies
Church of Scotland
CSV Scotland Community History Project, People's Story and Living Memory
    Association
Currie District Local History Society
Edinburgh, Leith and District Battalion, Boys' Brigade
J.S. Marr
Maureen Runciman
Stewart Skirving, Old Town Oral History Project
Alan Smith, Edinburgh Military Tattoo
The Scotsman Publications
Miles Tubb
Alan Willoughby, Secretary, Edinburgh Area Scout Council

The remaining pictures were taken by the author or are from his personal collection gathered over many years of loving his city.

Special thanks to my wife Mary for her assistance.